# Ice

By Julie Haydon

## Contents

# All About Ice

Ice is frozen water.

Ice is cold and hard.
Ice floats in water.

There is ice on the land
in some very cold places.

3

Rivers and lakes can freeze.
Sometimes, people skate on the ice.

The sea can freeze, too.
The ice can be very hard and thick.
Big animals can walk on it.

If ice warms up, it melts
and turns into water again.

Water can freeze,
then melt … then freeze … then melt.
Water can do this over and over again.

Ice can be any shape or size.

Ice is amazing
because it can turn into water very quickly.

# Experimenting with Ice

## Goal

To find out if ice melts more quickly in warm water or in cold water.

## Materials

You will need:

- paper

- a red, a blue and a green pencil

- two ice blocks

- a glass of warm water

- a glass of cold water

- a stopwatch.

## Steps

1. Draw a chart on the paper.

**2.** Put one ice block
in the glass of warm water.

**3.** Start the stopwatch.

**4.** Stop the stopwatch
when the ice has melted.

**5.** Write the time it took
for the ice block to melt on the chart.

**6.** Put the other ice block
in the glass of cold water.

**7.** Start the stopwatch.

**8.** Stop the stopwatch
when the ice has melted.

**9.** Write the time it took
for the ice block to melt on the chart.

## Observation

The ice block in the warm water
melted more quickly
than the ice block in the cold water.

## Conclusion

Ice melts more quickly
in warm water than in cold water.

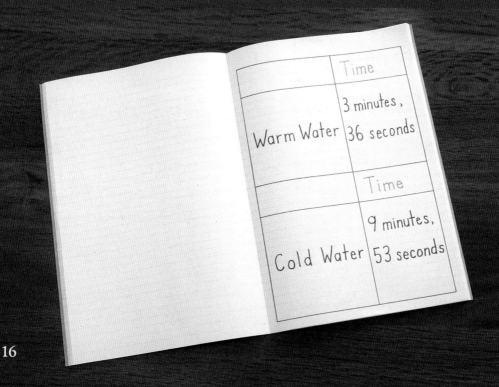

| | Time |
|---|---|
| Warm Water | 3 minutes, 36 seconds |
| | Time |
| Cold Water | 9 minutes, 53 seconds |